SWATCOM

SWATCOM

Tactical Communications
Manual for SWAT Operations

Tony L. Jones

PALADIN PRESS • BOULDER, COLORADO

SWATCOM: Tactical Communications Manual for SWAT Operations
by Tony L. Jones

Copyright © 1998 by Tony L. Jones

ISBN 0-87364-961-3
Printed in the United States of America

Published by Paladin Press, a division of
Paladin Enterprises, Inc., P.O. Box 1307,
Boulder, Colorado 80306, USA.
(303) 443-7250

Direct inquiries and/or orders to the above address.

PALADIN, PALADIN PRESS, and the "horse head" design
are trademarks belonging to Paladin Enterprises and
registered in the United States Patent and Trademark Office.

CONTENTS

LIST OF FIGURES

LIST OF PHOTOGRAPHS

ACKNOWLEDGMENTS

Many people provided technical information to make this book possible. Here is a rough list of people to whom I would like to send a heartfelt thank you:

Ed Jenks, representing Aisin World Corp. of America; H.D. "Dave" Krick, representing Braley Communication Systems; Andrew Ferguson, representing Carolina Ordnance; Chris Putnam, representing Ceotronics; William Moles, representing Defense Technology Corporation of America; Gary Wolfe, representing Dodgen Mobile Technologies Division; Lawrie Lewis, representing Horizons Unlimited; Devin R. Lee, representing New Eagle International; Robert B. Rosen, representing Remote Satellite Systems International; and Micheline DaMoude, representing Transcript International.

I also want to extend a special thank you to my wife, Kay, for her patience during many proofreadings and word processing efforts and for ignoring the aroma of my numerous cigars. (She may not believe cigar smoke is aromatic.)

Additionally, I wish to thank SWAT officer Barry McKinnon, a true professional. His consent to be a subject in many photographs contained in this book was a great help indeed.

Finally, I want to recognize the many officers who have experienced the breakdown of tactical communications. The fallen ones are past help; hopefully this book will help prevent the adding of names to "fallen in the line of duty" memorials.

PREFACE

A variety of tactical communication methods have been used to control military (tactical) operations for hundreds of years. Colorful uniforms used to designate units (clothing); guidons (flags); cannon fire, bugles, drums, and whistles (sound); smoke pots and aerial flares (pyrotechnics); runners (messengers); and so on were used before the invention of telephones and radios. And even after the invention and widespread use of these technological devices, earlier forms of tactical communication remained useful.

Technology can breed an overreliance on a specific system or item. Many SWAT teams depend too heavily on radio communications. Radios can and often do fail during tactical operations. This failure may be due to equipment breakage, weak batteries, "dead spots," power limitations, poor radio operating procedures, lack of training, adversary exploitation, and so on.

Lack or loss of communications will always cause a loss of control. SWAT operations are hazardous enough without conceding a measure of control loss during a mission. The amount of control lost will depend on the training level of the SWAT team and its proficiency in using alternative tactical communication methods.

Clear, secure, and accurate communication is critical during SWAT operations. It is what enables SWAT organizations to operate in effective teams. The intent of this book is to inform SWAT operators and familiarize them with the variety of communication methods that may be used during a tactical operation and examine the strengths and weaknesses of each. This book is certainly not all-inclusive; the methods available are limited only by the operating team's imagination.

Each communication method may be used in a stand-alone manner, in exigent circumstances as a backup, or in conjunc-

tion with other methods. Since there are strengths and weaknesses unique to each, the SWAT team's goal is to build a
strong communications program by capitalizing on communication strengths and avoiding inherent weaknesses. Remember,
strong, solid communication methods are fundamental to realizing strong, solid SWAT team control.

1

RADIO COMMUNICATIONS

Clear, secure, and accurate communication is an integral part of SWAT team tactics. All successful tactical operations consist of the proper mix of speed, security, and control. Each tactical operation is unique, requiring a different mix of these three elements in order to achieve success. Control is maintained by rapid, clear, concise, and accurate communications. The proper use of radios can be the most rapid and available form of communication utilized by SWAT teams.

COMMUNICATION CENTER

The highest level of radio communications is the base station found in police/security communication centers. The communication center is usually in a static location and serves as the main controller of all radios. However, distance and tactical necessity may require a communication center to be mobile. A mobile communication center serves the same purpose as the static communication center. Mobile communication centers are usually custom built on motor home chassis.

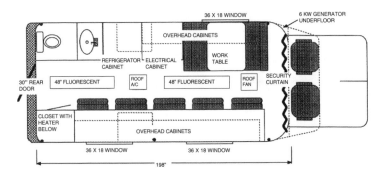

Figure A 24-foot Dodgen Mobile Command Unit Floor Plan #1.

1

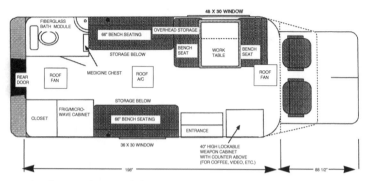

Figure B 24-foot Dodgen Mobile Command Unit Floor Plan #2.

Photo 1 Dodgen Mobile Command Unit.

MOBILE COMMUNICATION CENTER

The mobile communication center is often custom designed to serve as a tactical operations center. It may also serve as a command post, police substation, testing lab, surveillance center, catastrophe response center, and public relations vehicle. It should contain power adapters for base radios, hand-held radio battery chargers, cellular phones, computers, printers, faxes, and so on. There should also be a combustible fuel generator to serve as emergency or backup power in the vehicle. The mobile communication center's value is incalculable, but what happens if the vehicle breaks down or can't negotiate the terrain? The best solution is to equip the vehicle with removable/portable communications equipment. For example, Braley Communication Systems radios, faxes, cellular telephones, data ports, printers, and other such equipment (see Photos 2 through 5) are portable and designed to be set up using their own stand-alone battery source. All of the equipment is designed to fit into fully integrated hard shell cases for use in mobile environments. Each system weighs approximately 40 pounds. (See Chapter 4 to locate a Braley Communication Systems contact.)

Photo 2 ML 1000 Command Post Portable Cellular
Telephone/Fax/Notebook/PC/Printer Unit.

AST Notebook PC w/Fax Modem
Motorola 3 Watt Transportable Cellular Transceiver
AT&T Telephone
Cannon Bubble Jet – 10ex Printer
Ricoh PF2 Fax
Logitech Fotoman + Digital Camera (not shown)
12v Cigarette Lighter Adapter/110v AC/Battery Pack Power
Pelican Case
40 Pounds

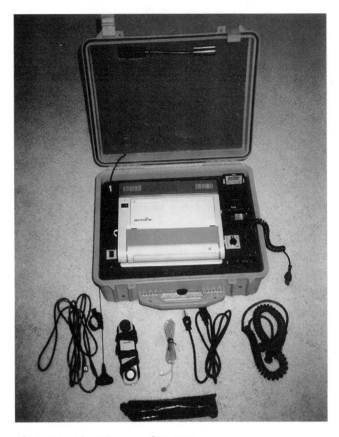

Photo 3 Incident Command Unit #1.

Mitsubishi "Access" Multifunction Fax
Motorola "Flip Phone"
Motorola 3-Watt Booster Kit for "Flip Phone"
Computer RJ11 Data Port
Battery/12v DC/110v AC Power
Pelican Dust/Waterproof Case w/Light
40 Pounds

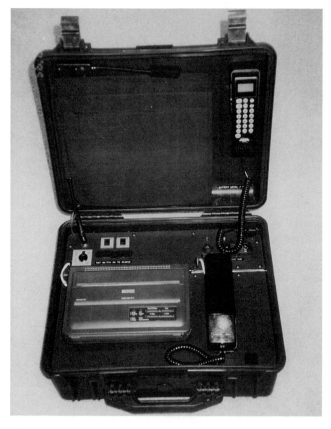

Photo 4 Incident Command Unit #2.

Ricoh PF2 Multifunction Fax
Motorola 3-Watt Cellular Phone
ATT 530 Telephone Handset (Cellular and/or Landline)
Cellular or Landline
Computer RJ11 Data Port
Battery/12v DC/110v AC Power
Pelican Dust/Waterproof Case w/Light
40 Pounds

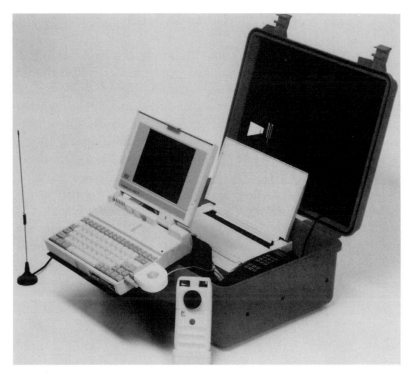

Photo 5 ML 950A Cellular Notebook and Camera Package.

Portable Cellular Telephone/Fax/Data Port Unit
AST Notebook PC w/Internal Fax Modem
Cannon Bubble Jet Printer
Logitech Digital Camera
Motorola 3-Watt Transportable Cellular Telephone
12v DC/Battery Power w/110v Charger
Pelican Dust/Waterproof Case w/Light
40 Pounds

HAND-HELD RADIOS

The next level of radio communications concerns hand-held units known as handsets, bricks, or portables. These units should be as portable as possible while containing the following basics: 5 watts of power, multichannel capabilities, encryption capabilities, flexible antenna, adjustable squelch and tone control, earphone and microphone jacks, channel monitoring capability, duress button, push-to-talk (PTT) button, and hands-free operation. The use of repeaters can extend the range of portable radios by boosting weak radio signals to their original power. When multiple repeaters are linked together or trunked, the radio signal is directed to the next available channel as soon as a radio unkeys. Trunking avoids the condition of hanging onto one channel waiting for a transmission to end. Radio signals are constantly moved to whichever channel is available. Trunking provides rapid access to free channels.

HEADSETS

For tactical purposes, headsets used in conjunction with PTT and voice-activated systems are essential. Headsets must be portable, secure, comfortable, adjustable, and lightweight. Many headsets use devices that clip on the ear or insert into the ear. They are usually uncomfortable and can cause ear irritation or infections, and they often fit poorly, which causes the earpiece to drop out continually. Also, when the earpiece is in place it prevents the operative from hearing noises on one side while operating in the tactical arena.

New Eagle's headset (fig. C) enables the user to hear transmissions through a vibrator that lies on the side of the face. The hollow bones in this area allow sounds to be heard. A flexible boom mike complete with windscreen is used to transmit. Push-to-talk buttons are located on an interface box, as shown in Figure D, or on a finger mount, as in Figure E.

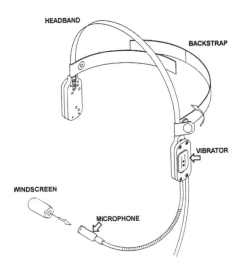

Figure C New Eagle International Headset.

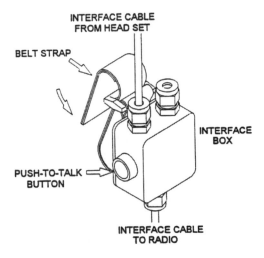

Figure D New Eagle International Interface Box.

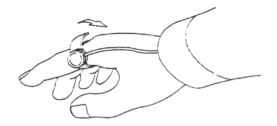

Figure E New Eagle International PTT Button, Finger Mount.

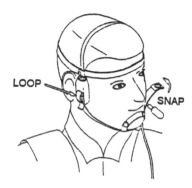

Figure F New Eagle International   **Figure G** New Eagle International Head
Head Strap System.   Strap and Chin Strap System.

An interface box is connected between the handset and head-set. The interface box can be fastened anywhere the operator chooses for convenient PTT button access. The finger switch is very convenient and flexible; it may even be fixed to a weapon. This system is also adaptable to most chemical protective (gas) masks that utilize voicemitters. Additional headset stabilization may be realized by using a head strap and/or chin strap (see figs. F and G).

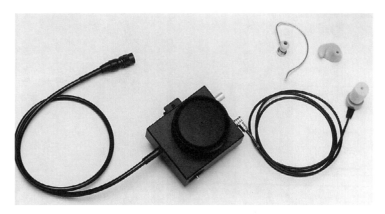

Photo 6 Ceotronics Contact-Com depicting three earpieces, PTT unit, and radio plug cable.

Another fine headset is the Contact-Com, made by Ceotronics. The Contact-Com uses a microphone that is housed in a small rubber boot that transmits the user's voice via bone conduction. The microphone rests on the operator's head and transmits voice vibrations generated through the top of the head. Transmissions are received through earphones, as depicted in Photo 6. The Contact-Com can be used in helmets, tactical headgear, or with protective (gas) masks, as illustrated in Figure H. The Contact-Com can be used in a stand-alone configuration with the custom-designed headband shown in Figure I. Transmissions are initiated by a PTT switch, shown in Photo 7. The strength of this system is the elimination of boom microphones and hand microphones, which enhances the user's flexibility. Figure J depicts the Contact-Com microphone, earphone, and push-to-talk button assembly. (Contact the manufacturer for a full explanation of the options available.)

Headsets can be plagued by the wires snagging on equipment. Operators should place wires under clothes or use the channels built into tactical vests. Operators must ensure that the wires are not too tight or their movements will be restricted. However, the wires must not be to loose, either, or they will snag on equipment, obstacles, or weapons systems.

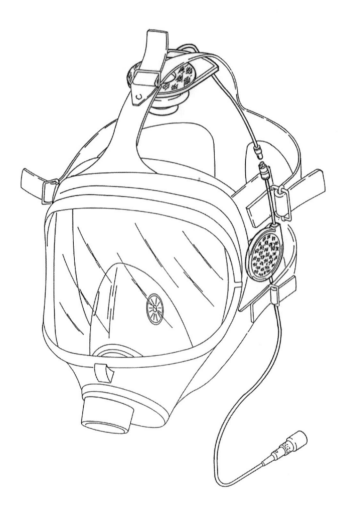

Figure H Contact-Com in Gas Mask.

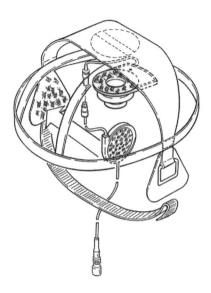

Figure I Contact-Com Custom-Designed Headband Unit.

Photo 7 Contact-Com Transmission Switch—one cable leads to the hand-held radio, the other cable leads to the headset.

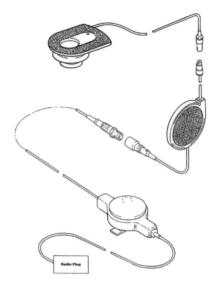

Figure J Contact-Com Microphone, Earphone, and PTT Button.

VOICE-ACTIVATED OPERATION

Some handset and headset systems contain a voice-activated transmission option. This means that noises of any type that the microphone picks up will be transmitted automatically. The microphones may be housed in boom mikes, throat mikes, or bone-conduction systems. The main problem with voice-activated microphones is their propensity to pick up interference (e.g., operators breathing heavily while under stress; ambient noise; and nonessential information such as general conversation, profanity, etc.). These sources of interference are magnified by the number of operators using voice activation. Push-to-talk operation is usually more efficient. Voice activation may be a useful option for snipers who want to use hands-free operations. Snipers usually operate in quiet environments and in two-man teams which observe strict noise discipline, therefore avoiding incidental noises.

RADIO CAPABILITIES

Radios, generally viewed as the primary means of communication employed in tactical operations, have many capabilities. Radios are mobile, and transmissions are instantaneous or real time. Radios are not affected by line of sight, as are other forms of communication. They allow an unlimited number of personnel in a variety of locations to receive and transmit information, and their transmissions can span great distances. Finally, radios are usually simple to operate.

RADIO LIMITATIONS

Radios have weaknesses as well. Radio transmissions can be intercepted, interfered with, or exploited by adversaries. Like all equipment, radios can break. Atmospheric conditions, electric lines, terrain features, or manmade sources can block or interfere with radio transmissions. (Areas where such interference occurs are called dead spots.) When scouts recon a target, they should note any dead spots and report them to the tactical operations center as well as the SWAT team leader. When several agencies are used in an operation, care must be taken to ensure that common frequencies, common power ranges, and compatible equipment are used. Radios shouldn't be used within 100 feet of any suspected explosive device, due to the possibility of electronic detonation. The most common reason for radio failure is probably weak batteries. Spare batteries must be carried in all tactical operations wherein radios will be a central part of communication methods.

PREVENTING ADVERSARY EXPLOITATION OF RADIOS

Adversary exploitation of radio communication is accomplished in three ways.

The first and easiest is by monitoring. Adversaries may overhear radio traffic by being close to the operator's external speaker. Monitoring may also be accomplished through the use of commercial scanners or a captured radio.

The second exploitation method is deception. To accomplish this, the adversary uses a captured or preprogrammed radio and transmits as a SWAT operator. The adversary may transmit false information and/or instructions; cause tactical operators to make unnecessary transmissions, thus tying up the radio network; or attempt to gather crucial tactical information such as the location of SWAT members. Adversary deception is made easier when SWAT teams do not have or do not follow radio operating procedures or when tactical actions are intense.

Jamming is the third method of adversary exploitation. Jamming is the deliberate interference with radio signals with the intent of disrupting communications in order to surprise, confuse, or mislead radio operators. It may be continuous or intermittent. There are generally two types of radio jamming methods that SWAT teams may encounter. The first is spot jamming, or the transmission of a narrow band signal intended to interfere with a specific frequency. The second is barrage jamming, which consists of transmitting a wideband signal intended to interfere with as many channels as possible. Jamming may be accomplished by keying a transmitter on the SWAT team's tactical frequency, thereby effectively blocking transmissions.

If jamming is suspected, the SWAT operator should, if possible, continue to function and never mention on the open net that jamming is suspected. He may increase transmitting power in an effort to overpower the jamming signal. The operator should also reduce transmission speed in order to talk through the interference. He may also adjust the handsets, fine tuner, and volume control. He may adjust the antenna in a clear area or relocate the radio to avoid natural and manmade interference. Finally, the operator may switch to a predesignated alternate frequency. A designated decoy operator may continue to transmit bogus information on the compromised frequency in order to trick the adversary into thinking his efforts are succeeding.

Monitoring may be avoided by using tactical headsets such as the New Eagle or Contact-Com. Adversaries will not be able to overhear incoming transmissions due to the proximity of the SWAT operator's ear to the receiver source. Nor will they be able to monitor the SWAT operator's transmissions because of the sensitivity of the boom, throat, or bone conduction microphones. These microphones are often sensitive enough to pick up a whisper. Of course, adversaries may monitor radio transmissions through the use of electronics.

Circuit Discipline

Minimizing Radio Traffic

Circuit discipline thwarts adversary exploitation by minimizing radio traffic (during tactical operations, only essential information should be transmitted). A well-planned mission reduces the need for transmissions. Nonradio means of communication also reduce transmissions. Avoid radio checks, time checks, and status checks as much as possible. Radio checks should only be performed at the beginning of a mission, when batteries have been changed or radio problems exist. Radio checks are designed to confirm the radio's status. Time checks are designed to periodically check a SWAT operator's location, status, or progress. These checks should be extremely limited. Status checks are designed to check on a SWAT operator's well being. They should also be extremely limited. The more radios that are used, the higher the chances that SWAT teams will be compromised. Remember, the number of operators x the number of radios = NOISE.

10 Series

Another rule of circuit discipline is to keep transmissions short by using short words, codes, or a 10 series. Codes are normally a substitute for whole sentences. For example, "Code 1" means, "I have arrived at my designated location." Another example would be code word "Dragon," which means, "Get ready, impending vehicle assault." The 10 series also represents short words. Table I depicts a sample 10 series.

TABLE I: SAMPLE 10 SERIES

10-99	-	Stop transmitting
10-98	-	Out of service
10-97	-	In service
10-19	-	Report to this station
10-18	-	Request for relief
10-17	-	Completed last assignment
10-16	-	Arrived at scene
10-15	-	In position
10-10	-	What is your location
10-4	-	OK/Acknowledgment

The 10 series can be limitless, and cards listing them should be disseminated to all SWAT members. It is the SWAT members' responsibility to safeguard this 10 series list. If a 10 series card is lost (compromised), a new one should be developed.

24-Hour Time Designators

To avoid the confusion of A.M./P.M. time frames, the 24-hour time language should be adopted. Table II shows this, and Table III shows how specific times translate to the 24-hour language.

TABLE II: 24-HOUR TIME

0000 = 12 A.M. (midnight)	1200 = 12 P.M. (noon)
0100 = 1 A.M.	1300 = 1 P.M.
0200 = 2 A.M.	1400 = 2 P.M.
0300 = 3 A.M.	1500 = 3 P.M.
0400 = 4 A.M.	1600 = 4 P.M.
0500 = 5 A.M.	1700 = 5 P.M.
0600 = 6 A.M.	1800 = 6 P.M.
0700 = 7 A.M.	1900 = 7 P.M.
0800 = 8 A.M.	2000 = 8 P.M.
0900 = 9 A.M.	2100 = 9 P.M.
1000 = 10 A.M.	2200 = 10 P.M.
1100 = 11 A.M.	2300 = 11 P.M.

TABLE III: 24-HOUR TIME TRANSLATIONS

1945 = 7:45 P.M.	0745 = 7:45 A.M.
1350 = 1:50 P.M.	0150 = 1:50 A.M.
1215 = 12:15 P.M.	0015 = 12:15 A.M.

Special Nets

Tactical operators should be assigned special nets or channels designated for tactical operations. No one else may use these channels except to transmit life-saving radio traffic. At a minimum, there should be a primary and a secondary channel set aside for SWAT use. This is why portable radios should be multichanneled. These SWAT channels alleviate nonessential radio traffic by streamlining users. If the primary channel is believed to be exploited by the adversary, SWAT members need only move to the secondary channel for secure communications. The switching of channels may be accomplished by code, 10 series, or a standard operating procedure (SOP). This SOP would state that upon command or adversary jamming, the SWAT operator will change to the next identified tactical channel. A radio check will have to be performed when channels are changed, in order to confirm SWAT members' compliance.

Transmission of Sensitive Tactical Information

SWAT members should avoid the transmission of sensitive tactical information in an effort to decrease the amount of information an adversary may use. Names of individuals, adversaries, hostages, SWAT team members, and so on should never be transmitted in the clear. Also, specific team designations (e.g., sniper teams, vehicle assault teams, entry teams) should not be transmitted in the clear. The teams should be given a code designator. For example, sniper teams could be called Sierra teams, vehicle assault teams could be called Victor teams, and assault teams could be called Alpha teams. Radios with encryption capabilities are valuable here. Encrypted radios scramble radio signals so that only specially coded radios can descramble the signal for coherence. All tactical radios should be coded and checked prior to a mission to ensure compatibility with encryption.

Radio Operating Procedures

Along with circuit discipline, radio operating procedures help thwart adversary exploitation.

Authentification System

The first procedure is the development of an authentication system. This system verifies messages as authentic when a challenge is correctly answered. If at anytime a SWAT operator suspects adversary deception, he must challenge the sender to authenticate. Tables IV and V illustrate authentication tables.

A challenge would be conducted as follows (see Table IV for reference):

call sign:
ENTRY TEAM LEADER = ECHO LIMA
SWAT COMMANDER = WHITE SNAKE

TABLE IV: NUMERICAL AUTHENTICATION TABLE

7 F	R	D	E	S	W	A
6 Q	G	T	H	Y	J	U
5 R	L	D	B	S	V	Z
4 K	I	L	O	P	Z	M
3 X	N	C	R	V	Q	A
2 P	L	E	D	I	J	T
1 H	R	N	W	G	L	E
1	2	3	4	5	6	7

TABLE V: ALPHABETICAL AUTHENTICATION TABLE

G 43	44	45	46	47	48	49
F 36	37	38	39	40	41	42
E 29	30	31	32	33	34	35
D 22	23	24	25	26	27	28
C 15	16	17	18	19	20	21
B 8	9	10	11	12	13	14
A 1	2	3	4	5	6	7
A	B	C	D	E	F	G

"Echo lima to white snake, over. "
"This is white snake, go ahead echo lima, over."
"Echo lima to white snake, I have one suspect down, over."
"White snake to echo lima, authenticate 4, 4, over."
"Echo lima to white snake, I authenticate Oscar, over."
"White snake to echo lima, roger, what is your location and situation report, over."

As can be seen, the authentication table is read to the right and up, as in reading a map. The authentication was correct. If authentication is incorrect, the SWAT leader may elect to gain a location on the adversary by falsely confirming the authentication, thereby deceiving the adversary. SWAT operators may then be sent to the given location in an attempt to neutralize the adversary. Authentication tables may be numerical as in Table IV, or alphabetical as in Table V.

Another way to use an authentication table is to authenticate a message upon transmission. For example (refer to Table IV):

call sign:
WHITE SNAKE = SWAT COMMANDER
ECHO LIMA = ENTRY TEAM LEADER

"Echo lima to white snake, over."
"This is white snake, go ahead echo lima, over."
"Echo lima to white snake, I have one suspect down,
    I authenticate 4, 4, Oscar, over."

The only way an adversary can break the system is by obtaining an authentication grid. If this breach of security is suspected, it may be corrected by adding or subtracting numbers or letters (see Table IV). The team leader may advise plus two for authentication. In this case, to authenticate 4, 4, read right to the numeral 4, then up to the numeral 4. The intersection point is the letter O, which in phonetics is Oscar. Now read two letters to the right of O and the authentication will read the letter Z, or Zulu in phonetics. Another way is to subtract at the beginning. In this case, 4, 4 is read by the operator going right to the numeral 2 since this is the correct designation derived from subtracting 2 from the first designated number, which was 4. Once the correct starting number is found, the operator reads up to the numeral 4, finding the intersection of I, or India in phonetics. Addition is always accomplished by going to the right, and subtraction is accomplished by going to the left. The briefing officer will explain and then require all SWAT operators to practice and demonstrate their understanding. A variety of addition, subtraction, color codes, and symbols can be utilized. The idea is not to overdevelop the system; a cumbersome, confusing table is counterproductive.

Care must be taken to avoid crowding the authentication table's margin, or a wraparound situation occurs. Crowding margins will cause the authenticator to run out of designators. For example, to authenticate 2, 2 minus 2, the correct authentication is Tango. Remember, subtraction goes to the left. The reader reads over to the numeral 2 and up to the numeral 2, which is Lima, but now two spaces must be subtracted, which are Lima and Tango, giving the answer Tango. This situation is prone to confusion, and unless all personnel are adept at using an authentication table it should be avoided. If a margin is over-read, a possible procedure is for the reader to transmit "authentication not valid."

A SWAT operator should never accept voice recognition as a substitute for authentication if he suspects that a message is false. Authentication should be pursued, and if a challenge is responded to slowly, a second challenge should be issued. Never use the same authentication combination twice, or you risk the possibility of adversaries writing them down. Combinations should be crossed out as they are used. Authentication tables are easily produced and should be pocket size and laminated for durability. These tables must be safeguarded and may be changed as required.

Procedural Words

Another radio operating procedure to consider is the use of procedural words, in order to reduce the length of radio transmissions. Table VI lists some common procedural words.

TABLE VI: PROCEDURAL WORDS

PROCEDURAL WORD	EXPLANATION/USE
ALL AFTER or WORD AFTER	This refers to the portion or word of a message that follows a certain word. This procedure is used to clarify a portion of a transmission instead of repeating a whole sentence or paragraph. For example: "One adversary has been located on side one <u>opening</u> two over." "Say again all after <u>opening</u>." The answer would be "two over," instead of the whole prior transmission.
ALL BEFORE or WORD BEFORE	This refers to the portion or word of a message that precedes a certain word. This procedure is used to clarify a portion of a transmission instead of repeating a whole sentence or paragraph. For example: "One <u>adversary</u> has been located on side one opening two, over." In response to "Say again, all before <u>adversary</u>," the answer would be "<u>one</u>," instead of the whole prior transmission.
AUTHENTICATE	This is a challenge issued to verify an operator's identity. For example: "Authenticate 4, 4." (See Table IV.)
AUTHENTICATION IS or I AUTHENTICATE	This answers the authentication challenge. For example: "Authentication is _____." (See Table IV.)

CORRECT

The transmission is correct.

CORRECTION

This is used when an error has been made in a transmission. The error may be one word or a series of words. For example, one word: "one adversary has been located on side one opening three <u>correction</u> two over." The all before or all after procedural words are used to correct a series of words. Using the examples above, the procedure would be "correction all after" (the operator states the last correct word) or "correction all before" (the operator states the first correct word). Example transmission: "One adversary has been located on side one opening three"— "Correction all after <u>located on</u> (side two opening two)."

DISREGARD LAST

The transmission is in error; ignore it.

DO NOT ANSWER

The operators called are not to answer in connection with this transmission. This procedure may be used to disseminate general information or announcements not requiring confirmation.

I SAY AGAIN

The operator is repeating a whole transmission or a portion of a transmission, indicated by the procedure words "all after" or "all before." For example, "I say again—all before _____." Or "I say again—all after

_____." The procedure is the same as when using "correction."

I SPELL

This is used to spell phonetically. For example: "I spell—**S**ierra, **N**ovember, **I**ndia, **P**apa, **E**cho, **R**omeo, over." Translation: SNIPER.

OUT

This signifies the end of a transmission, and no answer is required or expected.

OVER

This signifies the end of a transmission requiring a response. Once "over" is transmitted, it is OK for the receiver to transmit.

ROGER

This signifies the receiving and understanding of a transmission.

SAY AGAIN

The receiving member needs the last transmission repeated. Or if a partial message is received, the procedural words "all after" or "all before" can be used. For example, "Say again, all before (state last word.)" Or "Say again, all after (state first word)."

THIS IS

This transmission is used as a prelude to the identification of the transmitting unit. For example: "This is white snake." Confusion can easily result if a unit just transmits.

WAIT — ONE

The sender must pause for a few seconds before transmitting further. The net is still his.

WAIT — OUT	The sender or receiver must pause longer than a few seconds. The net is no longer his.
WRONG	This means the last transmission was incorrect. To identify a partially incorrect message, use the procedural words "all before" or "word before" or "all after" or "word after." For example: "wrong—all before (state first correct word)."

Duress Systems

If a SWAT operator has been taken prisoner or is in distress, a duress system should be initiated. Duress systems can be visual, written, spoken, or electrical. All duress systems must be planned to appear as natural as possible, in order to avoid adversary discovery. An example of a visual duress signal is flying the American flag upside down. A written duress system can be structured around uncharacteristic handwriting, unusual spacing, and the writing of a predesignated duress word. An electrical duress signal may be integral with the handset. This duress system consists of a button or pull-pin that, once initiated, transmits an emergency signal, giving a radio identity and sometimes a location. There should be a procedure in place to clear an inadvertent duress signal, such as a code word. If the duress signal isn't cleared, aggressive action to resecure this individual is required. The final type of duress signal is accomplished by using a code word. The code word can neither be apparent nor used in ordinary conversation. A balance must be sought. For example: The word "eat" is too common and will be overlooked. "Superman" may work, however. For instance, a SWAT officer is covered by an adversary's weapon, and when he sees another SWAT officer approaching, he may say, "Go cover your area, I don't need Superman." The other SWAT officer should now realize his teammate is under duress and should take applicable action.

Phonetic Alphabet

Another radio operating procedure to observe is the use of a phonetic alphabet (see Table VII for an example). The phonetic alphabet helps to prevent confusion and errors in radio transmissions. This alphabet is used to spell words that might not be understood if they were transmitted in the clear.

TABLE VII: MILITARY-STYLE PHONETIC ALPHABET

A = ALPHA	N = NOVEMBER
B = BRAVO	O = OSCAR
C = CHARLIE	P = PAPA
D = DELTA	Q = QUEBEC
E = ECHO	R = ROMEO
F = FOXTROT	S = SIERRA
G = GOLF	T = TANGO
H = HOTEL	U = UNIFORM
I = INDIA	V = VICTOR
J = JULIET	W = WHISKEY
L = LIMA	X = XRAY
K = KILO	Y = YANKEE
M = MIKE	Z = ZULU

A formal procedure to observe when using the phonetic alphabet is as follows: "I spell Sierra, November, India, Papa, Echo, Romeo, out." Phonetically, this spells sniper. The phonetic alphabet is used to disguise words, spell hard-to-pronounce words, or clarify words. Table VII illustrates a military phonetic system, but civilian versions may also be developed, as in Table VIII.

TABLE VIII: CIVILIAN-STYLE PHONETIC ALPHABET

A = ADAM	N = NORA
B = BOY	O = OCEAN
C = CHARLES	P = PAUL
D = DAVID	Q = QUEEN
E = EDWARD	R = ROBERT
F = FRANK	S = SAM
G = GEORGE	T = TOM
H = HENRY	U = UNION
I = IDA	V = VICTOR
J = JOHN	W = WILLIAM
K = KING	X = XRAY
L = LINCOLN	Y = YOUNG
M = MARY	Z = ZEBRA

As with a 10 series, if a phonetic system already exists, SWAT operators may wish to use it due to familiarity.

GENERAL RADIO OPERATOR PROCEDURES

In order to make the most effective use of radios, operators should be familiar with the radios' operating and maintenance instructions. The radios should be kept clean and dry. Regular maintenance should be performed to ensure that all plugs and jacks are clean, connections are tight, knobs turn easily, and batteries are fresh. The operator should speak clearly, distinctly, and directly into the microphone.

Radio Operator Training

SWAT operators should be trained to recognize the difference between adversary jamming and natural interference. This can be done by jamming radios during exercises and by finding dead spots or areas prone to interference to operate in. The SWAT officer should practice proper jamming circumvention. All codes, 10 series, military time tables, authentication systems, and duress systems must be known and practiced. The SWAT operator should practice the techniques of slowing down the message, saying words twice, and phonetically spelling out the words. The operator must also be familiar with the radio's strengths, weaknesses, operation, and maintenance procedures.

Proper training in conjunction with strict radio procedures will strengthen a SWAT team's tactical communications. Training also avoids horseplay. There is no place for improper radio procedures, e.g., profanity, noise-making, or cute phrases. Proper radio procedures reflect professionalism, good leadership, and strong SWAT teams. Improper radio procedures reflect novice operations, poor leadership, and weak SWAT teams. Remember, many people monitor radio transmissions, including police supervision, other police agencies, media, and ordinary citizens.

2

HAND AND ARM SIGNALS

Hand and arm signals represent words in the form of gestures and are an effective means of SWAT team tactical communication. These signals cut down on radio use, therefore decreasing the chances of adversary exploitation. Like all communication methods, hand and arm signals have advantages and disadvantages.

HAND AND ARM SIGNAL ADVANTAGES

Hand and arm signals require neither equipment nor power, nor can they be intercepted or exploited the same way as radio and telephone transmissions. An adversary must be very close to observe these signals. Even if he intercepts them, the adversary will have limited opportunities to use them. Chances are if he is this close he won't worry about hand signals but instead will engage the SWAT operator in weapons fire. Hand and arm signals are immediately received and transmitted (real time). They can be changed and new ones developed to meet mission requirements. The variations are limited only by the SWAT team's imagination.

HAND AND ARM SIGNAL LIMITATIONS

Hand and arm signals can be misunderstood. When even the spoken word can be misunderstood, it is easy to see how these signals can be as well. The use of hand and arm signals is restricted when line of sight is diminished (e.g., by darkness, smoke, fog, tactical formations, obstacles, chemical environment, etc.). And the distance over which these signals can be used is limited to the capabilities of the human eye.

EXAMPLES OF HAND AND ARM SIGNALS

The number of hand and arm signals available for use and the amount of information that can be conveyed are limited only by the SWAT team's imagination. Figures K through XX depict some examples of hand and arm signals.

"You"

The sending officer holds his arm outstretched and points his index finger at the receiving officer. The sending officer holds his weapon in the nonsending hand at the ready position.

Photo 8

Figure K

"Stop"
The sending officer holds his arm outstretched with the palm of the sending hand facing the receiving officer. The sending officer holds his weapon in the nonsending hand in the ready position.

Photo 9

Figure L

"Go"

The sending officer holds his arm down toward the ground so that it forms an "L" shape, then swings his arm from the rear forward. This movement indicates forward movement or "Go." His weapon is held in the nonsending hand at the ready position.

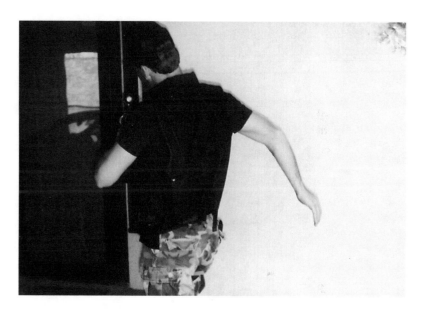

Photo 10

Figure M

"See" or "Watch"

The sending officer holds his hand in a horizontal position against his forehead, over his eyes. The weapon is held in the nonsending hand at the ready position.

Photo 11

Figure N

"Hear"

The sending officer holds his hand in a vertical position so that his thumb touches his head behind the ear; the palm of the sending hand faces the receiving officer. The weapon is held in the nonsending hand at the ready position.

Photo 12

Figure O

"Come"

The sending officer holds his hand and arm outstretched in front of his body, and he then pulls the hand and forearm toward his body, indicating movement toward himself. His weapon is held in the nonsending hand at the ready position.

Photo 13

Figure P

"There"

The sending officer holds his hand and arm outstretched, pointing his index finger at the place indicated. His weapon is held in the nonsending hand at the ready position.

Photo 14

Figure Q

"Around"

The sending officer extends his hand and arm in an "L" shape, horizontal to the ground. The hand and arm are moved from rear to front in an arc ending in front of the sender. This signal is often used in conjunction with "Go"—after the "Go" signal is completed the around signal is integrated. This would then mean "Go Around." His weapon is held in the nonsending hand at the ready position.

Photo 15

Figure R

"Enter"

The sender holds his hand and arm outstretched directly in front of his body, then swings his hand and arm rearward as if parting a curtain. His weapon is held in the nonsending hand at the ready position.

Photo 16

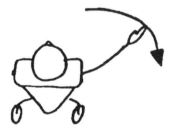

Figure S

"Numbers"

The sender holds his hand and arm in an "L" configuration even with his head. The desired number is indicated by the number of fingers projected. This hand and arm sign depicts the number 4. His weapon is held in the nonsending hand at the ready position.

Photo 17

Figure T

"Numbers—Addition"

The sender holds his hand and arm as depicted below. If the number 9 is desired, for example, four fingers would be projected, and then the hand is closed into a fist and five fingers are projected. The receiver knows to add four fingers and five fingers together, recognizing the number 9. This presentation must be slow and deliberate. The sender's weapon is held in the non-sending hand at the ready position.

Photo 18

"Message Received"

The sender holds his hand and arm outstretched, touching the tips of the index finger and thumb together. This is the traditional OK sign. His weapon is held in the nonsending hand at the ready position.

Photo 19

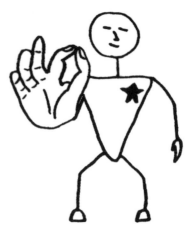

Figure U

"Unable to Understand"

The sender holds his hand and arm slightly bent, at shoulder level; the palm is facing up. The shoulder is then shrugged. His weapon is held in the nonsending hand at the ready position.

Photo 20

Figure V

"Yes"

The sender nods his head vertically up and down, in the traditional "Yes" motion. His weapon is held in the applicable firing position.

Photo 21

Figure W

"No"

The sender rotates his head horizontally from side to side, in the traditional "No" motion. His weapon is held in the applicable firing position.

Photo 22

Figure X

"Me," "I," or "Myself"

The sender points the index finger of his hand at the center of his chest. His weapon is held in the applicable firing position.

Photo 23

Figure Y

"Disregard"

The sender holds his hand in front of his body, palm facing the receiving officer, and then moves it from side to side, as if erasing a blackboard. The sender holds his weapon in the non-sending hand at the ready position.

Photo 24

Figure Z

"Suspect"

The sender encircles the wrist of his opposite hand as if grasping the suspect or simulating handcuffs. Even though his hands are together, the sender can easily fire his weapon as required.

Photo 25

Figure AA

"Hostage"

The sender grasps his neck with one hand, as if being choked. His weapon is held in the nonsending hand at the ready position.

Photo 26

Figure BB

"Shotgun (1)"

The sender holds his hand cupped inward at shoulder level in front of his body and moves it down and up as if operating a pump-action shotgun. The sender's weapon is held in the non-sending hand at the ready position.

Photo 27

Figure CC

"Shotgun (2)"

Another hand signal for shotgun is an expedient method for an officer who is carrying a shotgun. The sender just points at the weapon, signifying shotgun. His weapon is held in the non-sending hand at the ready position.

Photo 28

"Pistol"

The sender holds his hand to form the rough shape of a handgun by extending the index finger and bending the thumb. An alternate method is for the sender to point at his own handgun. The sender should have his weapon in the nonsending hand at the ready position.

Photo 29

Figure DD

"Female"

The sender holds a fist against his chest, indicating the enlarged breast of the female gender. The sender's weapon is held in the nonsending hand at the ready position.

Photo 30

Figure EE

"Male"

The sender uses the palm of one hand and strokes his cheek in a downward motion to indicate a beard for the male gender. The sender's weapon is held in the nonsending hand at the ready position.

Photo 31

Figure FF

"Door"

The sender uses the index finger of one hand to draw the outline of a door by starting out at an imaginary lower corner; extending the finger up, over, and down; and leaving the bottom open. The sender's weapon is held in the nonsending hand at the ready position.

Photo 32

Figure GG

"Window"

The sender uses the index finger of one hand to outline a window by starting at an imaginary lower corner and extending up, over, down, and across, making a box. The sender's weapon is held in the nonsending hand at the ready position.

Photo 33

Figure HH

"Automobile"

The sender holds a cupped hand in front of his body, rotating the hand in a half circle as if steering a car. The sender's weapon is held in the nonsending hand at the ready position.

Photo 34

Figure II

"Gas"

The sender places a hand over his nose and mouth. The sender's weapon is held in the nonsending hand at the ready position.

Photo 35

Figure JJ

"Automatic Weapon"
The sender places a hand held in a clawlike manner over the center of his torso and moves it up and down as if strumming a guitar. The sender's weapon is held in the nonsending hand at the ready position.

Photo 36

Figure KK

"Rifle (1)"

The sender extends an arm straight over his head, with the hand closed except for the index finger and the thumb, which are extended. The sender's weapon is held in the nonsending hand at the ready position.

Photo 37

Figure LL

"Rifle (2)"

An expedient method for signaling rifle can be accomplished by a sender who is carrying a rifle. He need only point at his rifle. The sender's weapon is held in the nonsending hand at the ready position.

Photo 38

"Sniper"

Using one hand, the sender encircles his fingers so they touch the thumb, then raises his hand to his eye as if looking through a rifle scope. The sender's weapon is held in the non-sending hand at the ready position.

Photo 39

Figure MM

"Cover Me"

The sender raises one arm over his head and bends his arm at the elbow, bringing the palm of his hand down over his head. The sender's weapon is held in the nonsending hand at the ready position.

Photo 40

Figure NN

"360-Degree Formation" or "Rally"

The sender raises one arm over his head, leaving his hand closed except for an extended index finger. The index finger is pointed up. The hand is rotated slowly in a circle. The sender's weapon is held in the nonsending hand at the ready position.

Photo 41

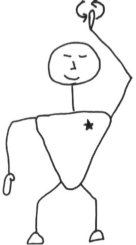

Figure OO

"Down"

The sender brings one arm out to his side, bending his arm at the elbow until his hand is horizontal to the ground, palm down. The sender's weapon is held in the nonsending hand at the ready position.

Photo 42

Figure PP

"Ammo"

The sender holds a magazine, speed loader, or round in one hand at head level, slowly waving the hand back and forth from the head to the outside of the arm. The sender's weapon is held in the nonsending hand at the ready position.

Photo 43

Figure QQ

"Silence"

The sender raises one closed hand to his mouth, with the index finger extended to touch his lips. The sender's weapon is held in the nonsending hand at the ready position.

Photo 44

Figure RR

"Hurry"

The sender raises one arm with his elbow bent to head level and his hand closed in a fist. He then pumps the arm up and down. The sender's weapon is held in the nonsending hand at the ready position.

Photo 45

Figure SS

"Dog"

The sender raises one arm to waist height and holds the hand palm up with all fingers separated and extended. The sender's weapon is held in the nonsending hand at the ready position.

Photo 46

Figure TT

"Line Formation"

The sender raises one arm horizontal to the ground with the palm down until it is chest high. The sender's weapon is held in the nonsending hand at the ready position.

Photo 47

Figure UU

"File Formation"
The sender raises one arm, bending it at the elbow. The hand is bladed with the palm facing the adjacent ear. The hand is then moved forward in a chopping motion. The sender's weapon is held in the nonsending hand at the ready position.

Photo 48

Figure VV

"Column Formation"

The sender bends his arm at the elbow and raises his hand until it reaches head level. The hand is closed except for two fingers held in a peace sign, which the sender moves back and forth, touching then separating. The sender's weapon is held in the nonsending hand at the ready position.

Photo 49

Figure WW

"Wedge Formation"

The sender holds his arm at an angle from the body with a closed fist, then moves the arm straight to the rear of the body. The sender's weapon is held in the nonsending hand at the ready position.

Photo 50

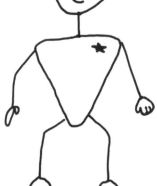

Figure XX

Hand and Arm Signal Series

This series of photos illustrates the use of hand signals in a series to communicate a full sentence. The sequence interpreted: "Stop—I see 4 hostages."

Photo 51

Photo 53

Photo 52

Photo 54

Photo 55

HAND AND ARM SIGNAL TRAINING

Hand and arm signals are chosen by frequency of use in operations. Remember, keep them simple. There are several ways to train SWAT team members in the use of hand and arm signals. Team members should demonstrate and practice each signal, and these demonstrations may be videotaped for use as a classroom refresher. Still pictures of each signal may be produced and used as flash cards. The SWAT member may then be tasked to identify each signal or arrange the pictures into a message. All hand and arm signals must be practiced until they are second nature. They must be given slowly, clearly, and correctly so they will not be misunderstood. Hand and arm signals should be developed for one-hand use instead of two. One-handed signals should not interfere with the emergency use of the operator's assigned weapon. These signals may be modified as required, but they need to be standardized so that everyone will be able to understand them if SWAT teams are integrated for an operation.

Hand and arm signals, as depicted in Figures K-XX, may stand alone to signal one word or be used in a series to signal a whole sentence, as in Photos 51-55.

3

ALTERNATE COMMUNICATION METHODS

There is a variety of nonroutine, less frequently employed communication methods. Many of these were used in a multitude of variations prior to the invention of telephones and radios. When used properly, these methods can enhance the flexibility, security, and effectiveness of the tactical communication process.

TELEPHONES

Telephones often serve as effective alternate, backup, or supplementary communications. There are generally two types of telephones to choose from—land line and cellular.

Land lines may be closed-circuit or open-circuit. Closed circuits are best described as telephones possessing no dial-in or dial-out capabilities. These telephones are connected to each other in a loop-type system. Closed-circuit systems are fairly rare for SWAT use except in industrial facilities. However, they may be used by hostage negotiators. The advantage lies in the no dial-in or dial-out capability. The adversary being negotiated with must not be able to call any audience, i.e., reinforcements, the media, etc., nor must he be able to receive calls from any outside parties. The hostage negotiator must control the telephone, not the inverse. The open-circuit telephone is by far the most common type of system. The open-circuit telephone may be made more secure by the use of scramblers and descramblers.

Cellular telephones are mobile due to their size, power source, and wireless design. These telephones are similar to radios, possessing many of the same capabilities and limitations. Due to the mobility of cellular telephones, they lend themselves to use by dismounted SWAT operators. Cellular telephones are less limited by obstacles than other forms of communication. This communication method is instantaneous, and the signal range can be

impressive when adequate
mobillink coverage is available.

Cellular telephones have
limitations as well. Since they
operate in a similar fashion to
radio transmission, they are
prone to adversary interception and exploitation. In urban
areas, there can be limitations
on signal range due to inade-
quate mobillink coverage.

A new cellular telephone
service called Skycell avoids the
conventional mobillink system.
Skycell utilizes a satellite called
the AMSC, owned by the
American Mobile Satellite
Corporation. The AMSC is the
most powerful commercial
communication satellite in the
world. The Skycell service is
combined with a Mitsubishi

Photo 56 SWAT Officer Using a
Cellular Phone.

ST151 transportable phone. The whole system is slightly smaller
than an average briefcase and expands cellular coverage to consist
of virtually all of North America, its surrounding coastal waters,
and the Caribbean. See Chapter 4 for a Skycell contact.

Telephone Capabilities and Limitations

Telephones have many tactical capabilities. Telephones are generally more secure than nonencrypted radio communications. They
allow person-to-person communication, streamlining the need-to-
know concept (access to tactical information). There is also the ability for either party to break in without waiting for a transmission to
be completed. Telephones are usually unaffected by terrain or
weather conditions. Minimal operator training is required for use.

However, telephones may be limited in certain circumstances.
The lack of mobility is a problem unless cellular telephones are avail-

able. Telephones can be exploited by adversaries. Adversaries may tap the lines, cut the wires, or jam the lines by calling the number and leaving the phone off the hook. Electronic countersurveillance techniques have improved dramatically since the South first used a tapping method on union telegraph lines during the Civil War.

Closed-circuit, open-circuit, and cellular telephones all possess strengths and weaknesses. SWAT teams must evaluate the strengths and weaknesses of closed-circuit, open circuit, and cellular telephone systems, then choose the one most applicable in each tactical operation. No one system is superior in every tactical operation.

PYROTECHNICS

Pyrotechnics are devices used for signaling, which, through burning, produce light, smoke, and/or noise. They are used to mark locations and to communicate prearranged signals. Their advantages lie in "real time" communications, i.e., the signal can be received as soon as it is sent. Examples include noisemakers; distraction devices, both hand-deployed and weapon-launched; smoke grenades, both hand-deployed and weapon-launched; smoke pellets; flares, both hand-deployed and weapon-launched; self-propelled flares; and tracer rounds.

Prior to using pyrotechnics, SWAT teams should consider some of their limitations. Pyrotechnics are limited by line of sight, obstacles, and poor visibility, any of which may negate their usefulness. Also, adversaries may see the devices and heighten their vigilance. Also, due to the burning-type initiation, fire is a hazard. For the most part, pyrotechnics are limited to outdoor use, and even then, precautions are required (i.e., fire department on standby, on-site fire extinguishers, etc.). A final limitation lies in their inability to be turned off once deployed.

Noise-Producing Pyrotechnics

12-gauge-shotgun and 37/40-millimeter launching systems can be used to deploy noisemakers.

Two 12-gauge rounds fall into this category. The first is called a bird bomb, originally designed as a wildlife-control device. When fired from a 12-gauge shotgun, this cartridge is propelled approximately 100 yards and then explodes, producing 120 plus decibels of sound. Another 12-gauge noisemaker is known as a whistle cartridge. Upon firing, this cartridge is designed to whistle from the shotgun's muzzle to approximately 100 meters. This one may be a good choice for use in residential areas, when loud explosive reports may cause panic or generate undue public/media concern.

The second round, the 37/40-millimeter noisemaker, is also known as the bird banger, for the same reason as for the 12-gauge bird bomb. Upon firing, the 37/40-millimeter bird banger travels approximately 100 yards and then airbursts with an extremely loud report. Figure YY illustrates a Defense Technology Corporation of America (DTCoA) 37mm gas launching pistol that can be used to launch the bird banger.

Distraction devices are designed to produce a loud report and brilliant flash upon detonation. These properties make them good signaling devices. As an example of their usage, take a sniper leader who is going to initiate fire-upon-command procedures. Realizing that radios may fail at a critical moment, he decides to deploy a backup distraction device. He gives the command to the sniper teams: "standby, ready, fire." As the sniper leader transmits the fire command over the radio, he simultaneously deploys a distraction device. The snipers will hear the fire command on the radio and/or hear the distraction device.

Remember, it is not just the sniper leader's radio that may fail, but the snipers' as well. Chances of radio failure are magnified by the number of radios used in an operation. Always use a backup means of communication. The likelihood of both the radio and the distraction device failing are remote. Both the DTCoA #25 Distraction Device (fig. ZZ) and the DTCoA Omni Blast 100 Distraction Device (fig. AAA) are hand delivered.

Weapon-launched distraction devices (fig. BBB) could be used in place of the hand-delivered device discussed in the previous scenario. These devices are usually fired from a 12-gauge shotgun and have a range of approximately 55 yards. For signaling purposes, an aerial burst would be most effective, but directional deployment can be performed as required.

Figure YY 37mm Gas Launching Pistol. (Source: Defense Technology Corporation of America.)

PRODUCT SPECIFICATIONS

Number of Shots: 1
Action: Single or double
Barrel Length: 8 inches
Overall Length: 12 inches
Weight: 3 pounds, 5.6 ounces
Sight: Breach block—50 yards
Frame: One-piece steel
Grip: Polymer-pistol type
Finish: Matte black
Applications: This launcher is a viable alternative for situations where other types of gas guns would not be practical. This gas pistol allows greater freedom of movement for the operator and may be carried in a holster or side bag. While this gas pistol can fire all of DTCoA's rounds, because of its barrel length, the 8-inch rounds may not perform as well as in other launchers.

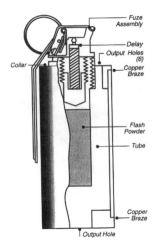

Figure ZZ #25 Distraction Device. (Source: Defense Technology Corporation of America.)

PRODUCT SPECIFICATIONS

Two-part reload and body.

Reload

Construction: Brass collar-cardboard tube
Fuse Type: M201A1
Sound Level: 174.5db at 5 feet
Light Level: 2,420,000 candela
Duration: 9 milliseconds

Body

Construction: Gun steel
Body Weight: 1.5 pounds
Body Shape: Cylindrical
Height Loaded: 5.73 inches
Diameter: 1.75 inches
Reusable: 25 times
Application: Signaling by loud report and brilliant flash. The possibility of physical damage or personal injury is minimal. However, if the gas ports are obstructed, the device may become airborne due to the energy directed toward the obstruction.

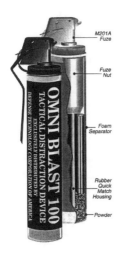

Figure AAA Omni Blast 100. (Source: Defense Technology Corporation of America.)

PRODUCT SPECIFICATIONS

Construction: Plastic
Explosive Compound: 19.5 grams smokeless powder and aluminum dust
Fuse: M201A1
Fuse Delay: 0.7-2.0 seconds
Sound Level: 175db at 5 feet
Light Level: 2,420,000 candela
Duration: 9 milliseconds
Height: 8 inches
Diameter: 1.5 inches
Weight: 9.5 ounces
Application: Signaling by loud report and brilliant flash. This device produces little smoke and is water resistant. Improper use can result in serious injury or death to the user and bystanders.

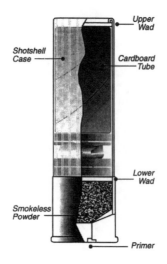

Upper
Wad

Shotshell
Case

Cardboard
Tube

Lower
Wad

Smokeless
Powder

Primer

Figure BBB 12-Gauge Diversionary Device. (Source: Defense Technology Corporation of America.)

PRODUCT SPECIFICATIONS

Diameter: 12-gauge
Length: 3 inches
Range: 55 yards (approximate)
Report: 100db at 50 yards
Application: Signaling by loud report. This round is intended for aerial deployment and should not be fired directly at personnel.

Smoke-Producing Pyrotechnics

Smoke grenades may be hand delivered or weapon launched. The payload is normally disseminated through continuous burning, as conflagration takes place. Figure CCC shows a DTCoA continuous-burning smoke grenade. Many smoke grenades are capable of being hand delivered or launched from 12-gauge shotguns or 37/40-millimeter grenade launchers. Figure DDD illustrates a DTCoA 37mm tactical launcher. Launching enables obstacle circumvention, directional deployment, and extended distance deployment. Depending on the weapons system used, smoke grenades may be launched from 90 to 300 yards. The 12-gauge projectile range is approximately 350 feet and will burn from 15 to 20 seconds. Figure EEE depicts a variety of DTCoA 12-gauge launching devices and cartridges. 37/40-millimeter smoke projectiles travel from 40 to 60 yards and will emit a steady smoke cloud for approximately 60 seconds. Figure FFF depicts a DTCoA 37mm smoke round. Smoke grenades are available in a variety of colors, e.g., white, red, green, purple, yellow, etc.

An example of using smoke as a signaling device is as follows: a SWAT team must cross an open field to set up on its objective. At 1600 hours, red smoke will be launched into this open field to both signal the assault and provide concealment for the team. Smoke pellets are ignited by a flame-producing device and are designed to generate a large amount of dense white smoke. They are the least convenient of smoke-producing pyrotechnics because of their lack of deployment options and ignition source.

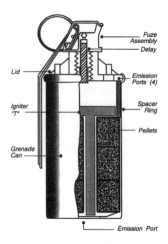

Figure CCC Continuous Discharge Grenade. (Source: Defense Technology Corporation of America.)

PRODUCT SPECIFICATIONS

Diameter: 2.6 inches
Length: 6 inches
Weight: 29.8 ounces
Fuse Type: M201A1
Discharge Time: 1.5–2 minutes
Launchable: Yes
Operation: Smoke is discharged through four ports located on top of the canister.
Application: This device should not be deployed onto rooftops, in crawl spaces, or indoors due to its fire-producing capability. It is designed for outdoor use. This device may be hand thrown or launched to approximately 90 yards. This device is launchable from a 37mm gas gun utilizing the #32 launching cup and the #36 launching cartridge or from a 12-gauge shotgun utilizing the #33 launching cup and the #35 launching cartridge. (See Figure EEE to view launching cups and cartridges.)

Figure DDD 37mm Tactical Launcher. (Source: Defense Technology Corporation of America.)

PRODUCT SPECIFICATIONS

Number of Shots: 1
Action: Single or double
Barrel Length: 14 inches
Overall Length: 18.31 inches
Weight: 5 lbs., 4 oz.
Sight: Breech block rear leaf, useable at 50-75-100 yards
Frame: One-piece steel
Grip: Polymer pistol type
Finish: Matte black
Application: This gas gun is used in tactical situations where the SWAT operator is unable to sight a shoulder gas gun due to situation restrictions. The pistol grip allows this platform to be fired from virtually any position. It is easily carried slung until needed for deployment. The tactical gas gun is capable of launching select DTCoA and other compatible grenades when used with DTCoA's #32 grenade launcher and #36 launching cartridge. (See Figure EEE to view DTCoA's launchers and cartridges.)

LAUNCHING CUPS

Specifications	No. 32	No. 33	No. 34	No. 100*
Weight:	15.26 oz. (436 grams)	9.56 oz. (273 grams)	8.58 oz. (245 grams)	5.95 oz. (170 grams)
Length (overall) :	7.75 inches	8.25 inches	7.25 inches	8.0 inches
Cup Diameter:	3.18 inches	3.18 inches	3.34 inches	1.60 inches
Material:	Aluminum	Aluminum	Aluminum	Aluminum
Fits:	37/38 mm Gas Gun	12 ga. Shotgun	12 ga. Shotgun	12 ga. Shotgun
Grenade:	No. 2, 3, 4	No. 2, 3, 4	No. 15 Series	No. 98
Product Code:	1390	1350	1380	1370

LAUNCHING CARTRIDGES

Specifications	No. 35	No. 36
Weight:	.48 oz. (13.7 grams)	1.93 oz. (55 grams)
Length (overall) :	1.94 inches	2.0 inches
Caliber:	12 gauge	37/38 mm
UN Number:	0014 Cartridges for Weapons, blank	0014 Cartridges for Weapons, blank
HAZ/COM Class:	1.4S Explosive Content: 4.21 grams	1.4S Explosive Content: 4.54 grams
Product Code:	1210	1270

The No. 35 and No. 36 Launching Cartridges are to be used with a 12 gauge shotgun and a 37/38 mm gas gun respectively. These are simply blank munitions to be used in conjunction with the appropriate launching cup to propel a specific grenade.

Figure EEE Launching Cups and Cartridges. (Source: Defense Technology Corporation of America.)

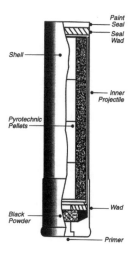

Figure FFF 37mm Smoke Round. (Source: Defense Technology Corporation of America.)

PRODUCT SPECIFICATIONS

Diameter: 1.5 inches or 37/38mm
Length: 5.5 inches
Maximum Range: 17 long range—150 yards
Maximum Range: 17 short range—75 yards
Discharge Time: 20–30 seconds
Total Weight: 7.9 ounces
Application: This round delivers smoke to target sites in the medium-to long-range classification. This smoke round is unstable and dispenses smoke by burning for 20 to 30 seconds. There is a definite fire potential, which mandates outdoor use only. It should not be deployed on rooftops, in crawl spaces, or indoors, nor should it be fired directly at individuals, since serious injury or death may result. When using smoke-producing pyrotechnics, SWAT teams must be prepared for a fire hazard and also consider wind direction. The wind can shift the smoke cloud so that it is of little value. Darkness may neutralize the function of smoke as well.

Flares

Flares are a valuable pyrotechnic that can be used in daylight or darkness. Flares can be hand delivered, hand launched, or weapon launched. Examples of hand-delivered flares may be common road flares that have varying burn rates or red magnesium ground flares. Red magnesium ground flares produce 15,000 candela, which is bright enough to light up one square acre for 60 seconds.

Hand-launched flares come in the form of self-contained, rocket-propelled flares. These flares are usually ignited by striking the rear end of the tube on a hard surface. The operator must be careful not to point this device at himself or anyone else. Upon ignition, the small, rocket-type propellant launches the flare approximately 750 feet into the air. The flare slowly descends under a small parachute canopy, burning for 40 seconds. These flares illuminate an area of approximately 250 to 300 square yards. Another hand-launched variation is the strobe parachute flare. This flare is rocket propelled and is deployed in the same manner as the aforementioned parachute flare and also ascends to approximately 750 feet. As this flare descends under its parachute canopy it provides a white strobe emitting approximately 350,000 candle power. The strobe impulse will illuminate 500 to 600 square yards for a period of 45 seconds.

Weapon-launched flares are designed around 12-gauge shotguns or 37/40-millimeter platforms. The 12-gauge flare will ascend to approximately 300 feet, emitting 14,000 candle power for eight seconds. 37/40 flares ascend between 300 to 400 feet, burning throughout their flight. Carolina Ordnance has developed a 37mm hand launcher that enables a SWAT operator to fire a variety of weapon-launched flares. Figure GGG depicts a DTCoA full-stocked 37mm launcher, and Figure HHH illustrates a DTCoA multishot launcher.

Two more flare launching systems are pen guns and flare guns. Pen guns launch a small red flare that will ascend to 300 feet, emitting 10,000 candle power for six seconds. These can be seen for approximately 19 miles on a clear night. Pen guns are reloadable. Flare guns are usually designed to fire 12-gauge flare rounds.

Figure GGG Full-Stocked 37mm Launcher. (Source: Defense Technology Corporation of America.)

PRODUCT SPECIFICATIONS

Number of Shots: 1
Action: Single or double
Barrel Length: 14 inches
Overall Length: 28 inches
Weight: 6.75 pounds
Sight: Breech block rear leaf effective at 50-75-100 yards
Frame: One-piece steel
Grip: Polymer-full stock
Finish: Matte black
Applications: This gas gun can fire all DTCoA's rounds plus other compatible 37/38mm munitions. It is also capable of launching select DTCoA and other compatible grenades when used with DTCoA's #32 grenade launcher and #36 launching cartridge. (See Figure EEE to view these devices.) The advantages of this gas gun are the 50-, 75-, and 100-yard sight increments, light weight, and strong stock.

Figure HHH 37mm Multi-shot Launcher. (Source: Defense Technology Corporation of America.)

PRODUCT SPECIFICATIONS

Operating System: Revolver-type, spring-motor-driven magazine with mechanically operated magazine stops

Safety: Trigger lock, out-of-line percussion cap to firing pin. The trigger pull brings the round into line with the firing pin before releasing the hammer.

Capacity: 6 shots

Ammunition: All 37/38mm ammunition up to 8.2 inches in length

Overall Length: Folding stock closed—20.5 inches
　　　　　Folding stock open—31.5 inches
　　　　　Fixed stock—32.75 inches

Weight Unloaded: 9 pounds

Barrel Length: 9 inches

Rate of Fire: Maximum six rounds in three seconds

Ejection: Shells drop out when frame is opened and tilted downward; sticky shells may be removed by hand

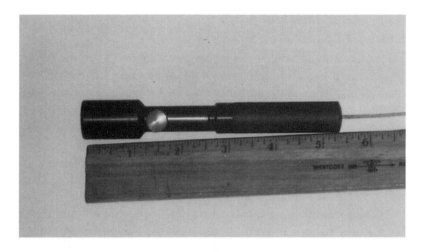

Photo 57 The pen flare gun shown is approximately 5.5 inches long and is made of steel. It is loaded by placing a flare in the belled end and fired by pulling the silver knob to the rearmost position and then releasing it. A spring-driven firing pin strikes the flare, launching it. The string in the far end is used as a lanyard.

Situations where flares may be used are vehicle assaults, open-air assaults, and building assaults, simultaneously initiated upon radio plus flare deployment. A radio signal would be transmitted and a flare would be deployed to initiate the tactical operation. Once again, the more radios in use during an operation, the greater the chance that some will fail. A visual backup deployed in the air for all to see is insurance of communication. Flares may also serve as a diversion when fired away from team locations. Adversaries will normally look at the flare and thus away from the SWAT team's location. SWAT operators should not look directly at a flare since this will destroy their night vision for approximately 30 minutes.

Tracer Rounds

The final pyrotechnic to be discussed is the tracer round. These are lethal rounds used to communicate to team members an adversary's location or to signal the impending expenditure of ammunition. For example, when a SWAT team operator sees the location of an adversary that other SWAT team members can't locate, he will communicate by firing a tracer round into the adversary's location, effectively marking it for all to see. To signal low ammo, SWAT operators can load their magazines so that the last three rounds fired will be tracers, providing them with a visual signal to reload prior to running empty.

When marking adversary locations, the SWAT operator must know the tracer round's capabilities. For example, a military 7.62 (.308) tracer round will burn for approximately 900 meters. A 9mm Hornady Vector burns out at approximately 98 meters.

Tracer rounds may be obtained from either military or civilian sources. Military tracers generally burn red, while civilian versions usually burn white. Communist bloc tracers usually burn green. SWAT teams must exercise restraint and discretion when considering the use of tracers due to the probability of starting fires.

Remember, all of these pyrotechnics can cause death or serious bodily harm if used improperly. They are not toys or fireworks. Follow all of the manufacturer's warnings and instructions.

LIGHT SIGNALING

Light can also be used for sending messages. Light signals offer the advantages of silence and ease of use through simple equipment. Their primary disadvantage is limited use due to short range, bright daylight, obstacles, and the mandatory development of a prearranged code. In addition, adversaries may see these signals, thereby increasing their awareness that something is happening in the tactical arena.

Some examples of lights that can be used for signaling are

as follows: flashlights, lasers, strobe lights, vehicle lights, spot-lights, building lights, and cyalume light sticks.

Flashlights

Flashlights come in a variety of sizes, powers, and lens colors (i.e., red, blue, and white). Size is not indicative of power. Compact flashlights, such as the Sure-Fire shown in Photo 58, offer as much or more candlelight power than many multicelled C or D battery models. The flashlight should be compact and fitted with a push-button switch. Push-button switches are usually easier to handle than slide or twist locking switches when sending signals. When flashlights are used to send signals, colored lenses may be used to convey meaning. For example, a white light means "stand by," a red light means "assault," and a blue light means "stand down."

The option of an infrared lens filter, an extremely useful feature, is available with the Sure-Fire flashlight. Infrared light is light that is invisible to the human eye. Thus, SWAT teams using night vision devices may send signals that are invisible to adversaries (unless they too have night vision equipment).

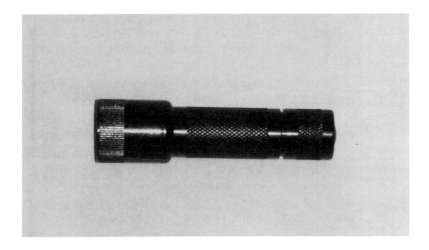

Photo 58 This compact flashlight has a push-button switch, adjustable beam, and may be fitted with a variety of accessories.

Another example of signaling entails turning the light on or off with a push-button switch. One flash means "stand by," two flashes mean "assault," and three flashes mean "stand down." Additional ways to send messages with flashlights include pointing one stream of light at a prearranged object and tracing figures. For example, pointing one stream of light at a preselected door means "assault," while moving the light in a box figure means "stand by." SWAT operators must control light beams to avoid splashing their bodies with light, thus creating a halo-like effect. Remember, keep all signals simple, and brief SWAT operators on their source and meaning.

A word of caution regarding weapon-mounted flashlights: these lights should only be used for signaling in exigent or strictly controlled circumstances. The operator is pointing a weapon where the light is pointing. The operator must never point a weapon at anything he isn't willing to destroy. Extra batteries and flashlight bulbs must be available for replacement as required. Batteries and flashlight bulbs may become inoperative with little or no warning.

Lasers

Lasers are used to communicate by projecting a concentrated beam of red light. Depending on the system used, the range will be from 15 to 700 yards. These distances are diminished by bright light sources, e.g., sunlight, smoke, and chemical irritant environments. The operator must follow all of the manufacturer's warnings, especially the requirement of avoiding eye exposure to the laser. Lasers may be weapon-mounted or hand-held. Weapon-mounted lasers should only be used for signaling in exigent or strictly controlled circumstances. Remember, where the laser goes, the weapon's muzzle goes.

Hand-held lasers in the form of laser pointers are a communications choice. The beam may be pointed at a prearranged object to send a message. For example, the laser beam projected on a window marks an adversary location. Remember, like tracers, lasers work both ways. The SWAT operator using a laser is marking his own location as well. The SWAT officer should send the signal from behind cover and then move to a new location.

Photo 59 This strobe light is compact, waterproof, made of plastic, and is powered by a dry cell battery.

Strobe Lights

Strobe lights emit bright white light impulses that are 350,000 candle power or more. From the air, strobe lights can be seen for miles. Strobe lights are best used for marking a location. For example, one could be thrown in front of an adversary's location. This procedure marks the adversary's location, destroys his night vision, and may distract him. Strobe lights will operate for many hours on a fresh battery. Another use is to mark landing zones for helicopter extraction of wounded personnel and such.

Vehicle Lights

Vehicle lights, such as headlights, spotlights, turn signals, emergency flashers, and light bars, may be used for tactical communications. Care must be taken in planning and in using these lights because they are ubiquitous at all emergency scenes. Their use must be very clear, coordinated, and well planned, or the communication effort will be lost or misunderstood because of the presence of numerous similar sources. Designate one vehicle, in one location, to use a variety of signals in an effort to communicate. For example: the patrol car located on the one/two corner of the target house will turn on a spotlight that is pointed straight up into the sky, plus press the headlight dimmer switch five times in five-second intervals to initiate the building entry. The communication must remain simple but distinct from all other like sources. As can be seen, just directing a patrol officer to turn on his lights won't be sufficient. How many patrol cars present will have their lights on and how many will arrive with their lights on? Also what lights are to be used? Be careful when using communication methods that may be confused with similar sources.

Hand-Held Spotlights

Spotlights are similar to flashlights procedurally when sending signals. Like flashlights, spotlights can be used to send signals through the use of colored lenses. (For example, red light means "stand by," blue light means "assault," and white light means "stand down.") Spotlights may be vehicle-mounted or hand-held. Power sources derive from a vehicle battery or a self-contained battery. Switches are usually a continuous type. If this is the case, shades can be used to flash signals. Any item that is dense and large enough to prevent light escape can be used as a shade. For example, the sender would cover the spotlight's lens, turn the light on, and then alternately uncover and cover the lens, simulating a flash. One flash means "stand by." Additional messages are sent by using the shade to simulate flashes. The spotlight's lens must be covered before turn on and turn off functions, or the light may be seen as a flash, confusing the message.

Spotlights are valuable when powerful lights are required. Their biggest limitations are their large size and propensity to become very hot.

Structural Lights

Building or structural lights may be used to send tactical messages. These lights include outside and inside lights. For example, a SWAT team has formed at its entry point and is awaiting the "assault" signal. The SWAT team leader has been briefed to watch a porch light on the house next door for this signal. The "assault" signal will be the turning on and off of the porch light three times. Other possibilities are room lights, floor lights, perimeter lights, and so on. It is usually best to signal by operating the lights in an unusual manner, such as turning them on and off several times in fairly rapid succession. (Don't operate the lights too fast, however, or the signal may be confusing and/or misinterpreted.) The reason for this is to prevent the possibility of confusion should someone inadvertently turn the lights on in the affected area. This is of particular concern in industrial complexes, where there may be a wide variety of locations from which personnel can access light switches.

Cyalume Light Sticks

A final source of light-operated communications is the cyalume light stick. Cyalume light sticks consist of chemicals housed separately in plastic tubing. To initiate the light stick, the tube is bent until an inner container snaps, causing the chemicals to mix and create a composition that glows. Full illumination is realized by shaking the device vigorously for a second or two. Cyalume light sticks are available in a variety of colors (red, yellow, green, blue, white, and infrared), sizes, and glowing times. Cyalumes are best used in short-range situations because of the limited amount of light produced. Also, a cyalume carrier is a good idea, because once a cyalume is activated it can't be shut off. The carrier is a tube housing the cyalume stick that when rotated exposes or conceals the light source.

Cyalume light sticks are utilized with color schemes (e.g., red means "assault," yellow means "stand by," and so on). Signals may also be sent by using the cyalume carrier or by concealing and exposing the device a specific number of times in a gear bag. For example, the operator opens the carrier then closes it to simulate a flash. With a gear bag, the SWAT operator initiates the device in the bag, pulls the device out to display it, then places it back in the bag. This represents a flash. Flashes represent signals (e.g., one flash = "stand by," etc.).

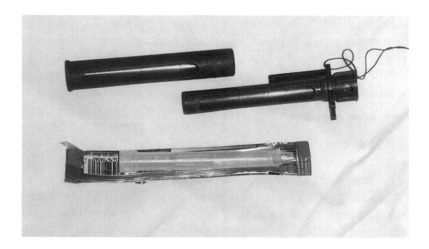

Photo 60 This cyalume light stick is lying on the original wrapper. The carrier is made of plastic and comes in two pieces. To use the carrier the two pieces are pulled apart, and the cyalume light stick is activated and inserted into the hollow tube. The piece with the knurled knob is now inserted and twisted to cover the open slot. To expose the light stick, the knob is twisted to expose the open slot. A lanyard is attached to hang or tie the device on gear as desired.

Cyalume light sticks require no battery source and are waterproof. The infrared light, invisible to the human eye, is excellent for SWAT teams using night vision devices because it will be invisible to adversaries unless they too have night vision devices. (Of course, this is a distinct possibility, considering the availability and low cost of Russian night vision devices on the open market today.)

ALTERNATE VISUAL COMMUNICATIONS

There is a variety of alternate visual means of tactical communications—visual signals that do not require mechanical parts, electronic parts, or a power source. Examples are mirrors, flags, clothing, appearing or disappearing personnel, windows left opened or closed, vehicle formations, and so on. These signals

ALTERNATE COMMUNICATION METHODS   **103**

depend on line of sight, careful planning, and careful execution. Normally adversaries will not recognize these signals as such.

Mirrors
Mirrors can be used to reflect sunlight in the form of flashes to send a message (e.g., one reflection or flash means "stand by," etc.). The use of mirrors is limited to bright sunlit days and may be difficult to maneuver toward the receiver's location. Because of these limitations, mirrors should only be used in exigent circumstances.

Flags
Flags are another means of visual communication. Different colors can be used to send various messages. For example, a red flag means "assault," and so on. The positioning of a flag can also send a message. However, often flag poles won't be available except perhaps at businesses or industrial complexes, and their location may make them unusable. Flags may be lowered by ropes from rooftops or windows. The use of flags is limited by line of sight, available display locations, and available colored cloth. Prefabricated flags may be stored in a tactical vehicle in an effort to make them more available.

Clothes
Clothes can be a method of visual communication. If the signaling person appears wearing an orange traffic vest, it means "assault;" if he is wearing a yellow raincoat it means "stand by," and so on. During interdepartmental tactical operations, clothing such as colored ball caps, police stenciled coats, and colored windbreakers can be used to communicate the identities of SWAT operators versus adversaries. Another variation is the appearance or disappearance of a signaling person. For example, if the signaling person is sitting in a vehicle and then lies down, disappearing from view, this means "stand by." If he gets out of the vehicle and enters a building, it means "assault," etc. A signaling person should be located in sight of SWAT operators but out of the adversary's sight.

Windows

SWAT operators can send visual signals by opening or closing windows. For example, if all of the windows facing a SWAT team on an adjacent building are closed, one window opened means "stand by," two windows opened means "assault," and so on. The inverse could be initiated if all of the windows were open, e.g., one window closed means "stand by"; two windows closed means "assault"; etc. The signals to be sent may be limited to certain windows. For example, in Figure III, the signal for "assault" is the closing of any two second floor windows, and in Figure JJJ the signal for "assault" is the opening of any two second floor windows. In Figure KKK, however, two second floor windows must be closed in sequence to signal "assault," and in Figure LLL, the "assault" signal is two second floor windows opened in sequence. If windows cannot be opened, curtains or blinds can be opened or closed to send signals in the same way.

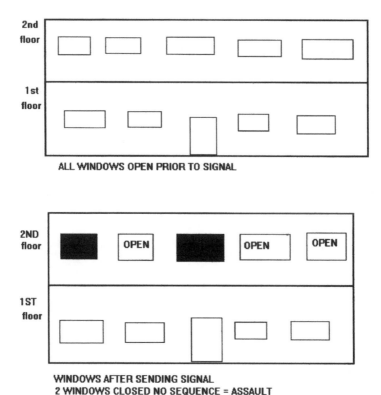

Figure III Closed window signals—no sequence.

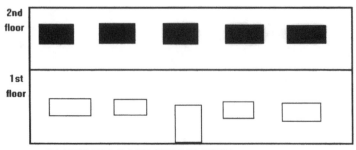

ALL WINDOWS CLOSED PRIOR TO SIGNAL

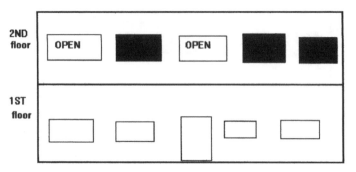

WINDOWS AFTER SENDING SIGNAL
2 WINDOWS OPEN NO SEQUENCE = ASSAULT

Figure JJJ Open window signals—no sequence.

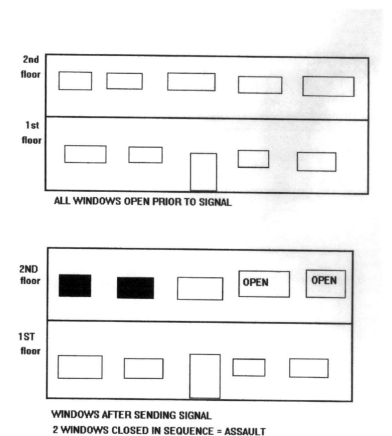

Figure KKK Closed window signals in sequence.

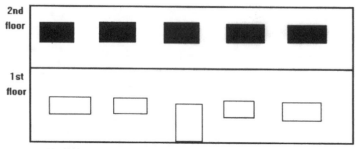

ALL WINDOWS CLOSED PRIOR TO SIGNAL

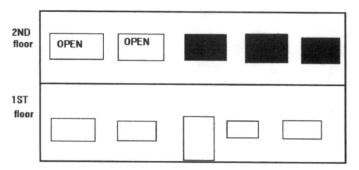

WINDOWS AFTER SENDING SIGNAL
2 WINDOWS OPEN IN SEQUENCE = ASSAULT

Figure LLL Open window signals in sequence.

Vehicles

A final method of visual communication is performed by the predesignated positioning of a vehicle or vehicles in formation. For example, a vehicle parked in a certain place, such as on the corner of a predesignated building, means "assault." To add clarification, a certain configuration may be added, for instance, opened rear doors and trunk. So the symbol for assault becomes a vehicle parked at the corner of a predesignated building with both rear doors and the trunk open. Formations may be set up by mixing vehicle types or by using like styles. An example of a mixed formation to communicate "ready" is to park two cars and a truck by a predesignated dumpster. By contrast, a like-style formation might be three squad cars parked in a line formation next to a predesignated tree to communicate "assault." Use the vehicles that are currently available; there is no need to request special vehicles for signaling purposes.

SOUND COMMUNICATIONS

Sound communications are available to all SWAT teams. Sounds other than those produced by radios or pyrotechnics can also be used as a means of tactical communication. Some examples include loudspeakers, bullhorns, whistles, bells, sirens, horns, intercoms, finger snapping, and so on. These can often be disguised to sound like routine noise and will be recognized as signals only by a trained listener. Sound signals are used to attract attention, give an alarm, or convey prearranged messages. These signals must be distinct and simple in order to prevent misunderstanding. SWAT operators must be aware that sound signals are effective only over short distances. They can be intercepted and/or interpreted as signals by an adversary, and they may also be distorted by adversary-produced sounds or ambient noises.

Loudspeakers

Loudspeakers are used to disseminate information quickly to large groups of people. Loudspeakers may be internal, such as hailing systems; external, such as bullhorns; or vehicle-mounted, such as public address systems in patrol car light bars. A big disadvantage is inherent in the dissemination style itself. No information that may be useful to an adversary can be broadcast due to the possibility of adversary interception.

Whistles

Whistles can be used effectively in sound communications. For example, one blast means "stand by," two blasts mean "cease fire," and so on. Whistles allow the sender to communicate more loudly than is possible with voice commands, and they are generally compact, fitting easily into a pocket.

Bells

Bells are located in many industrial complexes and can easily be used to communicate prearranged signals. Bells will usually have to be used in a sequence. For example, a two-bell sequence means "assault," and so on.

Sirens

Sirens, like bells, are located in most industrial complexes and can be used to communicate prearranged signals. Emergency vehicles have sirens that can be used for signaling as well. Signaling may be accomplished by using a certain tone (e.g., warbling) or sequence (e.g., two siren blasts). Prearranged siren signals must be distinct and known by SWAT operators. A drawback is that sirens can be easily drowned out or distorted by other arriving or departing emergency vehicles.

Horns

Horns are available in many industrial complexes. These horns are often air-operated types, which are loud and may be used to send prearranged signals, such as two horn blasts to mean "assault." Several repetitions are required in order to avoid confusion with normal horn operations. Another type of horn available in nearly all tactical arenas is the emergency vehicle horn. These can be used in the same way as air horns to send prearranged signals. However, as with sirens, vehicle horn signals must be distinct and known by SWAT operators. Vehicle horns can easily be drowned out or distorted by other emergency vehicles.

Intercoms

Intercoms are another choice for sending messages by sound. Many businesses, industrial complexes, and some homes have intercoms. Naturally clear voice communications are not an option due to the possibility of adversary monitoring. However, code words, music, or a variety of noises can be used to send a message to SWAT teams. For example, the sender might access the intercom and verbalize a prearranged signal by announcing, "A personnel accountability is in progress; all personnel report to the Sierra Bravo." In this case, "Sierra Bravo" means "stand by," because the phonetic alphabet was used to designate the first letter in each word. This signal must be prearranged and unrecognizable to an adversary. Playing music or making noise on an intercom can serve the same function. An example would be the SWAT operator tapping his fingers on the intercom microphone slowly, in sequence. However, care must be taken to avoid alerting the adversary.

Finger Snapping

Another method of sound communication available to all operators is finger snapping. For example, a SWAT operator snaps his fingers two times, which means "attention." Finger snapping is only useful in quiet environments where the SWAT operators are close together. Adversaries can hear finger snapping only when they are very close to the SWAT team. If this occurs, the least of the SWAT team's worries will be adversary interception.

Verbalization

A final example of sound communication is verbalization. Verbalization is used to communicate with team members and adversaries. Verbalization is used within the SWAT team to shout orders, directions, or warnings as required. When SWAT operators verbalize with adversaries, they should order compliance, not ask. The SWAT operator should use short words or sentences to avoid adversary confusion. Long, rambling directions are hard to deliver when under stress. The adversary, who is also under stress, will have a hard time complying with complicated directions. Only one SWAT operator should verbalize with the adversary, in order to avoid multiple conflicting directions. Usually, the first contact officer will issue necessary directions. Short words and sentences avoid the struggle between mental and physical tasks. Words and sentence structure require cognitive processes just as physical actions do. Choosing formal words and forming long sentences may delay a SWAT operator's motor skills (e.g., shooting). Remember, an adversary will already have the edge in the action-versus-reaction contest.

Finally, profanity should be avoided. Profanity is neither intimidating nor impressive. To the contrary, it is unprofessional and may be detrimental when the scenario is reflected upon in the courtroom. The use of profanity also adds useless words to the verbalization process.

MESSENGER

The final alternative communication method to be discussed is the messenger. The messenger is the most secure means of tactical communication. The only way an adversary can intercept the communication is by capturing the messenger. The chances of this transpiring are very remote. A messenger may be stopped by adversary weapon fire, but even then message interception or exploitation is unlikely. The adversary would have to secure and search the messenger's body, again unlikely during SWAT operations. The messenger is the best means of delivering lengthy documents, maps, photographs, and so on.

Certain limitations present themselves when using a messenger for tactical communications, however. Verbal messages may be misunderstood, misinterpreted, or incomplete when recited from the messenger's memory. Therefore, the sender should always write down messages. In addition, the messenger's speed depends upon transportation available, adversary observation,

Photo 61 The messenger delivering blueprints.

adversary fields of fire, physical conditioning, terrain features, and weather conditions. A major limitation of this form of communication is the lack of direct person-to-person conversation. For example, once documents or a verbal message have been delivered, it may be beyond the messenger's ability to answer questions. The messenger must then carry these questions back to the original sender, requiring answers to be carried back to the original recipient. Communications by messenger are costly in terms of manpower, time, and training.

CONCLUSION

Contrary to what is commonly believed, radios are not the only form of tactical communications. All of the communication methods discussed are designed to be used in backup or support situations. No method should be chosen as a sole source of tactical communications. A combination of at least two means of communication should be planned for each tactical operation.

Tactical signals must be simple, distinct, clear, and included in the warning order and/or operation order. All SWAT operators must be informed of each signal's meaning or the signal will be worthless.

SWAT teams should develop various forms of communication and practice them until they are second nature. Each SWAT operator should be trained in the use of different communication methods. Lack or loss of communications will always cause a loss of control. The amount of control lost will depend on the training level of the SWAT team.

4

EQUIPMENT SOURCES

The following is a list of contacts for a variety of special equipment covered in this book. This list is not intended to be all-inclusive. The procurement officer or recommending officer should always contact factory representatives to request demonstrations and test samples and conduct field evaluations prior to purchase. It might be possible to obtain a list of current product users from manufacturers, sales reps, and customer/subscriber lists of law enforcement product catalogs and professional periodicals in order to research product performance in a wide variety of environments and circumstances. Avoid haste when choosing equipment. Most departments operate under strict budget constraints that require a one-chance option at procuring the best equipment. A dangerous state of affairs can result when poor or improper equipment is selected. Never choose equipment by appearance, Hollywood hype, or image alone.

COMMUNICATION HEADSETS AND SYSTEMS

Ceotronics
2312 Trinity Mills Road
Suite 101
Carrollton, TX 75006

New Eagle International
100 1/2 Madore Street
Silver Lake, KS 66539

FLASHLIGHTS AND SYSTEMS

Laser Products
18300 Mt. Baldy Circle
Fountain Valley, CA 92708

MOBILE COMMUNICATION CENTER/EQUIPMENT

Aisin World Corp. of America (AWA)
10916-4 Moorpark Street
Los Angeles, CA 91602-2258

Braley Communication Systems
4088 Sugar Maple Drive
Danville, CA 94506

Dodgen Mobile Technologies Division
Highway 169 North
P.O. Box 39
Humboldt, LA 50548

SATELLITE TELEPHONE SERVICE

Skycell
1010 Lootens Place, #17
San Rafael, CA 94901

SIGNALING MUNITIONS

Carolina Ordnance
1985 Tate Blvd., SE
Suite 614
Hickory, NC 28602

Defense Technology Corp. of America
P.O. Box 240
Casper, WY 82602-0240

Horizons Unlimited
P.O. Box 426
Warm Springs, GA 31830

Hornady Manufacturing Company
Box 1848
Grand Island, NE 68802-1848

TELEPHONE SCRAMBLER/ENCRYPTORS

Transcript International
4800 NW 1st Street
Lincoln, NE 68521-9918

ABOUT THE AUTHOR

Tony L. Jones has more than 13 years of experience in SWAT operations and nuclear security plus 23 years of military experience. Much of Jones' experience has been in training and management positions. These positions include Shift Commander, Communications Captain, Shift Field Captain, Response Team Leader, SRT Commander, Sniper Leader, Sniper Commander, Firearms Instructor, SRT Training Officer, Security/Tactical Consultant, Training Director, Assistant Security Chief, and Special Deputy.

Mr. Jones served in the army, Army National Guard, Air National Guard, Air Force, and Army Reserve a total of 23 years.

His military service includes positions as a Fire Team Leader, Squad Leader, Assistant Platoon Sergeant, Military Police Supervisor, Security Police Supervisor, Security Police Liaison, Air Base Ground Defense Instructor, Small Weapons Instructor, SWAT Instructor, Training Coordinator, and Operations Training and Readiness Specialist. A Desert Storm Veteran, he achieved the rank of Master Sergeant and is a member of the Air National Guard Senior NCO Corps.

Mr. Jones is a published

author and has written four books titled *Booby-Trap Identification and Familiarization, SWAT Leadership and Tactical Planning, SWAT Sniper: Deployment and Control,* and *SWATCOM: Tactical Communications Manual for Swat Team Operations.* He has written more than 60 articles for the following publications: *American Survival Guide, Calibre Press, Command, Gun World, Law Enforcement Technology, Law and Order, S.W.A.T., The Call Out, The Chief of Police, The Firearms Instructor, The Informed Source, The Police Marksman, The Police Shield, The Police Supervisor,* and *The Tactical Edge.* In addition, he has written more than 150 lesson plans focusing on police/security tasks and serves as a staff writer for *The Police Shield* newsletter, a nationally distributed publication.

Mr. Jones graduated *Cum Laude* from Ohio University with a bachelor's degree in criminal justice. He also holds an associate's degree in business management (*Magna Cum Laude*) from Southern State Community College, and an associate's degree in industrial security (*Magna Cum Laude*) from the Air Force Community College. Tony is currently pursuing a master's degree in defense management.